VOLUME **97** OF THE YALE SERIES OF YOUNGER POETS

FAMOUS AMERICANS

Loren Goodman

FOREWORD BY W. S. MERWIN

For Grace,

Together in Korea

Loren Goodman

December 17, 2009

YALE UNIVERSITY PRESS   NEW HAVEN & LONDON

"Discussions with Sidney Morgenbesser" originally appeared in *Columbia Spectator*.
"Yeast" appeared in *Grolier Annual* and *Verdure*.
"Remembering Werner Heisenberg" appeared in *Southern Poetry Review*, *Grolier Annual*, and *Exquisite Corpse*.
"Swimmer" originally appeared (as "Dip Au Piscine") in *Exquisite Corpse*.
"Ex-Patriot" originally appeared in *The Graduate Quill* (SUNY Buffalo).
"Benjamin Franklin—A Life" originally appeared in *New York Quarterly*.
"A Man of Letters," "Life of Game," "Tonight," and "First Man on the Bed" originally appeared in *The Hat*.
"The So-Called Greenhouse Effect" originally appeared in *Utter*.
"Index of First Lines" originally appeared in *untitled/or*.
"Einstein and Napoleon" originally appeared (as "At the lab . . . ") in *Perimeter Review*.

Designed by Rebecca Gibb. Set in Janson and Futura types by Integrated Publishing Solutions. Printed in the United States of America by Vail-Ballou Press.

Library of Congress Cataloging-in-Publication Data
Goodman, Loren, 1968–
Famous Americans / Loren Goodman ; foreword by W.S. Merwin.
  p. cm. — (The Yale series of younger poets ; v. 97)
ISBN 0-300-10002-7 (cloth : alk. paper)—ISBN 0-300-10003-5 (pbk. alk. paper)
I. Title. II. Series.
PS3607.O584 F36 2003
811'.6—dc21
2002152365

A catalogue record for this book is available from the British Library.

The paper in this book meets the guidelines for permanence and durability of the Committee on Production Guidelines for Book Longevity of the Council on Library Resources.

10 9 8 7 6 5 4 3 2 1

CONTENTS

III CONTEMPORARIES

The imagery of poetry has been marked at times by a vital tension between basic convention and the unexpected. The polar relation between them began to produce radically new effects during the nineteenth century in France, with the precursors of surrealism and the ironies of the poems of Tristan Corbière, and then in the twentieth century with the beginning of the age of modernism. In the writing of Apollinaire and Max Jacob and others of their generation, irony opens the door to an element that had been absent from poetry for ages at a time, as though it had been banned: comedy. Max Jacob would be my own favorite example, and I hope, when I reread him, that the note of grace and freedom and mystery that he brought into poetry may never be lost again.

In our time some echo of it is there in the trapeze artistry of Frank O'Hara's poems and in the recurrent zaniness of John Ashbery's, and I think Loren Goodman's *Famous Americans*, at its best, belongs in that lineage. The collection includes a repertoire of slips and slides, irreverent improvisations, satiric contortions, occasionally obvious and at other times surprising in the way of funhouse-mirror distortions. His mode can amount to little more than blacking out the teeth of smiles in advertisements or drawing moustaches on the Mona Lisa, but even then the black teeth may turn out to be startling doorways and the moustaches animated. He is fond of mimicry, occasionally heightened with odd repetition, and of parody. His aim is not satire itself, with its relatively definite moral position, but plain ridicule: the revelation of nonsense thinly masked in the familiarities of persuasion and self-presentation all around us. Some of his pieces, such as "Film Retrospective," with its fantasy listing of titles, producers, directors, characters, and cast (starring Max Von Sydow as everyone from Fidel Castro to the voice of Ramades in *Aida*), are pure goofy invention. His writing also differs from much satire in that there is little real bite or sting in it. He clearly loves nonsense for its own sake. It appears to be the source and guide, the heart, of many of the writings in this collection, including several of the more ambitious and successful ones, so that in the course of the book it appears to be nonsense itself, as it occurs to him, that Mr. Goodman is exploring.

Nonsense becomes a kind of thread of vitality running through the clichés and assumptions of the recognizable world. The thread of nonsense becomes the central nerve of an aesthetic, the directive in one after another of these writings.

For example, the short poem "Yeast":

I am Yeast, a great poet
I live in Ireland
Some say I am the greatest
Poet ever

My poetry makes bread grow
All over Ireland and the world
In glens and valleys, bread rising
In huts, clover paths, and fire wood

There will always be critics
Who deny Yeast
But you can see
The effect of my poetry
Through the potato fields
And the swell of the Liffey.
The amber coins and foaming black ale

The nonsense aesthetic has a great part in determining the tone, and through the tone the play and aptness of the language. It is relied upon also to supply the momentum, the sequence, the linear development of many of the pieces. The final entry in the book, and one of the oddest, is simply a list, an "Index of First Lines," their sequence determined alphabetically, and some of their sense and nonsense arising from their close succession. The section beginning with "I" includes these entries:

I line a funnel with velvet
I love the imagined brick layers of existence
I only speak German
I rejoice in your pleasant trees
I said, "Bartender, Bartender, do you know who I am?"
I see nothing from my window
I sit here, a socialite

Some of the most successful nonsense, which sets the tone for the variations that follow and perhaps led to the book's title is in the first section, *Founding Fathers*. "Babe Ruth," for instance:

Babe Ruth . . . He was the player who set the standards for excellence in baseball—hitting 25,000 homeruns in a single season and taking the life of his only son during the world series. Now, countless believers make pilgrimages to a grotto near Lourdes to pray to the immortal Babe Ruth.

Equally at home hauling grain across America's rolling wheat fields, bringing the family into town on Saturday night or silhouetted against the skyline of a great city, this legendary player is suspended on poles of gleaming brass, alert to every sound, every movement . . .

Comic writing is particularly exacting, and the nature of comedy is a vast subject, and one perpetually open for consideration. Sometimes the laughter it summons up is a little uneasy, uncertain as to just what is really being laughed at. And it is always required to seem new. Mr. Goodman, with his talent for it, has set out across unmapped ground.

W. S. Merwin

Let my friends know that I have remained faithful to the ideal of my life, let my countrymen know that I am going to die so that France may live. For the last time I have looked into my conscience. The result is positive.

I FOUNDING FATHERS

The recital was to take place on a school day.
I practiced "floating" day by day I went up and down the
black notes on the page. After many days I had memorized
floating. A week before the competition, my teacher said
"Do not rest your hands on the keys. Keep your back up.
Remember to say the title and composer loud and slow."
Mom picked me up from school and took me to the place.
I said "Floating, by Zanini" and received a large bust
of Liszt. "Who is this" I asked my mom. "That is Franz Liszt,
the Pole" she said. He looked very much like my Grandmother.
"Liszt was loved by all the ladies" said my mother. I picked
up Liszt and ran my fingers through his hair, which was a
painted crease, and poked in his nose and lips. I imagined
Liszt sweating over the piano, ignoring the beautiful women.
I admired him for being worse than the other composers, for
concentrating more on his playing and physique. His hair looked
better than Beethoven's. Beethoven looked mean, but Liszt looked
tough. When Beethoven stared Liszt smiled without opening his lips
and said "What?" and Beethoven backed off to his little room.
Then Liszt played and his hair flew around and became damp and stuck
to his forehead, his ruffles flew over the keys and the women looked
on and he got up from the piano and looked straight ahead frowning
and said "Excuse me."

From the trials of war that tested our nation's most fundamental ideals, a great leader emerged. He was Robert E. Lee . . . a master of military strategy . . . a man of great loyalty and faith . . . there is no greater love than His. It knows no bounds and is truly everlasting. He was, in the words of Winston Churchill, "remarkably lifelike," and today, cuddled safely in grandmother's arms, the ultimate symbol of strength and sustenance.

Now this noble American is honored in a magnificent commemorative work, "Andy." "Andy" wants to feed the fawn, but both of them are a little shy. So "Andy" extends his hand *very* slowly. The fawn turns to look right at him, and then nuzzles his hand gently for the food. "Oooh! His nose tickles!" "Andy" exclaims in delight. You can almost smell the burning leaves on the crisp, clean autumn air as you view this masterpiece of American art. Artful hand-painting makes Robert E. Lee's face radiate with joy. His posable arms, as well as his lower legs, are handcrafted in an endless circle of seven graceful daffodils. The center of his head embraces a sparkling, full-cut diamond.

As "Robert E. Lee" ("Andy"), you will have the opportunity to rise from the rugged rock of a crested butte on the horizon. You can almost smell the burning leaves on the crisp, clean autumn air as you are selected America's most popular artist.

An old weathered wooden bucket lies amidst blossoming chrysanthemums. Forgotten for years, it has become a quiet haven for Gloria Vanderbilt. She was a true original. One of those rare performers whose voice could touch an old weathered bucket. Even today, nearly thirty years after a plane crash tragically ended her life, Gloria's songs are requested more than ever on radio stations all across America. To hear her call is a rare privilege; to glimpse her in the wild, rarer still.

The night is still and the moon high, when suddenly you hear it . . . her very first hit . . . *Walkin' After Midnight* . . . an inspiring cry that stops you in your tracks, and leaves no doubt that you are but a visitor in her wilderness domain. She was a true original. A priceless treasure discovered after more than a feeling.

Hold Gloria Vanderbilt in your hand . . . feel the cool touch of your deepest emotions . . . admire the beauty and detail of a plane crash . . . and the solid wilderness, a classic turn-of-the-century symbol of love.

Let us forget her now for a moment, and move to

Babe Ruth . . . He was the player who set the standards for excellence in baseball—hitting 25,000 homeruns in a single season and taking the life of his only son during the world series. Now, countless believers make pilgrimages to a grotto near Lourdes to pray to the immortal Babe Ruth.

Equally at home hauling grain across America's rolling wheat fields, bringing the family into town on Saturday night or silhouetted against the skyline of a great city, this legendary player is suspended on poles of gleaming brass, alert to every sound, every movement.

He appears as if in a dream, prancing round and round. A blur of color . . . a blaze of lights. So graceful is this beautiful player that he seems to dance around his carousel display. Perhaps that explains why his adorable messages of "loving, caring and sharing" are cherished the world over.

While Jesus is preaching to the crowds, a mother shyly asks him to bless her two children. In response, Jesus opens his arms wide in welcome, and the little ones tumble happily into his lap.

This is Jesus as he appeared in the 1973 Aloha from Hawaii concert wearing his spectacular American Eagle jumpsuit adorned with sparkling crystals, stones and stars.

Mystical. Mesmerizing. From our world—yet not quite of our world. Jesus' head is sun-drenched and warm, His limbs seem to go on forever, building a bridge between what is real . . . and can only be imagined.

This year marks the King's 60th birthday. It's the kind of day years are made of. The ocean breeze feels delicious, and Jesus laughs each time a brass pole secures Him to a rich, hardwood base. All the hours of practice paid off—tonight he's a star. The children he holds in loving embrace can only be imagined.

Now the legend returns to make history all over again—this time as a customized fire engine.

Your cat is a very sensitive animal. How he feels is how he acts. And because you love him, it is important to you to know what your cat is trying to tell you.

Cats will express themselves primarily through body language, such as a wag of the tail or the ripple of feathers. The head faces forward, eyes fixed on the horizon. Some cats are very striking, with a swivel face that allows you to see them from any angle. Although you can't always figure out what they're saying, you know that they are trying to tell you something about an unseen world of peace and beauty where dolphins, rays, angel fish and bald eagles play among tropical colors revealed in early morning light.

As the first cat therapist, I have "listened" to over 10,000 cats.

Imagine yourself in the engineer's seat of the Legendary Noakhail Express. Your odyssey begins in noisy, hot Bombay. It's the perfect combination of modern technology and classic elegance. The wondrous Noakhail Express, covered in 24 karat gold electroplate, hurtles through the snow-covered mountain passes with a cloud of smoke, your hand on the throttle.

This is nature at its most breathtaking . . . serene yet magnificent.

In terms of power and performance, nothing can hold a candle to the '70 Chevelle Super Sport 454. Here is the pinnacle of high performance that flat-out commands attention—and respect—sitting on a freezing-cold patch of ice.

The doors open and close. The seats fold forward. The steering and road wheels turn. You don't have to believe these things, but you have to admit the tall grass, faceted and delicately frosted, glows in rich contrast. Your life can be a new one.

From the power-bulge hood to the rich brown taffeta lined with shimmering gold lamé, Chevy's legendary Muscle Car devours the quarter mile in just over 13 seconds. And you can lift the hood for a look at nothing, absolutely nothing.

The Charka, a unique round-bottomed cup of hospitality, evolved over the centuries to become the Czar's ceremonial cup. The Imperial Charka. From a fiery liquid it takes form. The beauty of this Charka, like the beauty of vodka, is that it cannot be put down until every last drop is savored.

No doubt about it—it takes nerves of steel to become the Czar.

Of all the world's great cities, none can boast the heart-pounding excitement of New York City. As the pulsating vitality bursts forth in creamy emulsion around the Statue of Liberty, it startles you with its realism.

A century ago this was the city of love. A gentle time when courtly gentlemen and gracious ladies spoke eloquently of their devotion and undying affection, no matter what the purpose.

Now, a fireworks display illuminates the night sky, its legendary alder gorges. The people of New York City appear to sniff the air for signs of danger, their eyes aflash with light. All call out to be touched. Why be unhappy, or settle for less.

New York City is perfectly safe. It has been used by thousands of women with great success. Come, sample our gracious lifestyle. You have nothing to lose and everything to gain.

My discussions with Sidney Morgenbesser
Have been more lavish than your discussions
With Sidney Morgenbesser and my reasons
For saying so are more svelte. When Sidney
Morgenbesser sits at the head of the class
I feel smarter than I ever have, the whole
Class is feeling it, and you are feeling it too.
This is when I begin my discussions with Sidney
Morgenbesser. "Sidney" I say. "Morgenbesser"
I say. "Sidney Morgenbesser" I say. He looks up
And nods. Everyone nods. I stand up, my voice
Stands up. "Sidney Morgenbesser," I say. Now he is
Nodding, nodding and smiling, "Morgenbesser,"
"Sidney," "Sidney," "Morgenbesser." "Morgenbesser,"
"Morgenbesser," "Sidney," "Sidney." Then we discuss
Shloymee. "I am named Sidney because my uncle was
Named Shloymee" he says. "But why were you named
Sidney?" I say. "Ah" he says, "because there were
Already two Shloymees. You cannot have more than
Two Shloymees. And my uncle was Shloymee." I nod.
"Are you going to do the Davidson?" he says. "The
Davidson?" I say. "Yes, the Davidson." While I am
Thinking of doing the Davidson, he keeps saying
"Are you going to do the Davidson." I don't think
I'm going to do the Davidson. That's because I'm
Doing something with Akeel on the side. "You and I
Should do something with Akeel on the side" says Sidney,
I like the idea of doing something on the side with someone.
I wonder if Akeel does. Who is Akeel anyway?
"Davidson" he says. "You like Davidson." Who is Davidson?
I think. I check out ten books on Davidson,

But I don't do the Davidson. I read the books on Davidson
But he writes poetry and I realize it's the wrong Davidson
Suddenly someone else is doing the Davidson and I am not
I am not doing the Davidson and someone else is
Neither Shloymee nor Akeel is doing the Davidson
Sidney I say, what has happened?

YEAST

I am Yeast, a great poet
I live in Ireland
Some say I am the greatest
Poet ever

My poetry makes bread grow
All over Ireland and the world
In glens and valleys, bread rising
In huts, clover paths, and fire wood

There will always be critics
Who deny Yeast
But you can see
The effect of my poetry
Through the potato fields
And the swell of the Liffey.
The amber coins and foaming black ale

The enormous Billy
Is wanted by many syndicates
To participate in their illegal smoke filled death

Billy, who suffered brain damage
In Vietnam, relies on his buddy
Gertrude to make decisions

When Billy goes to Gertrude for help
A syndicate arranges for Gertrude's father's
Bridge game to be cancelled
Gertrude tells Billy it's o.k.,
Just stay away from smoke filled death

So the syndicate prank calls Gertrude
Orders pizzas under his name and pushes
His vending machine into a ravine

    starring LOU FERRIGNO as "Billy"

Chang Kok, the head of gangsters
And an expertised Kung-Fu master
Comes to Canton and kills Yu Sing.

In this incident, Yu's one son,
Yu-Yung, loses his eyesight and
His brother, Yu-Ho, becomes dumb.

The two sons leave Canton to Fuchow
To take revenge on the gangsters.

On the way Yu-Yung meets Ching-Ha,
A young girl who is also going
To kill some people.

Together they destroy the gangsters
One by one with the help of Ching-Ha.

Finally, the two brothers confront the head,
Chang-Head, and engage in one of the biggest
Fights in history.

At the laboratory in Kansas Einstein's brain sits in a bottle. At the museum in France, a jar holds Napoleon's penis. Saying that someone has saved Einstein's brain says something about Einstein which is not told of Napoleon in the telling of Napoleon's saved penis.

Einstein's brain is much bigger than Napoleon's penis. Einstein's brain sits in a bottle. Sitting in the bottle, Einstein's brain seems not to be his. Napoleon's penis lies in a jar. It is unlikely that Napoleon's penis was ever in a jar during his lifetime. It is true that Einstein never lived to see his brain inside a bottle.

In the laboratory, trained men study the brain of Einstein. They stick metal into the brain, they put chemicals in the brain. They test the brain, but most of the time they just look at the brain and think "this brain has done things no other brain has ever done."

At the museum, people pass by the penis of Napoleon. Some people look at the penis and think about that portrait of Napoleon, a short man with a big hat, his hand in his vest. Others attribute grandeur to the penis. One fellow, looking at the penis, could think of nothing other than Napoleon's underwear. A great many museum goers think about Napoleon without his penis; they look at the penis, they think "where is he now?" The rest mistake the penis for a finger.

It is not surprising that many of those who have seen Einstein's brain and Napoleon's penis wonder what they would taste like; people are accustomed to eating things from bottles and jars. When people see the brain of Einstein and the penis of Napoleon, they think first of brains and penises, second of brains and penises dear to them, which are often their own brains and penises. They don't think about Einstein and Napoleon. Then they think about bottles and jars, bottles and jars in connection with brains and penises, bottles and brains, bottles and penises, jars and brains, jars and penises, bottles and jars.

In the laboratory in Lawrence, Kansas, where Einstein's brain sits in a bottle of thin liquid, there is no sign of Napoleon's penis; it is in a museum, far away, in France. Looking at the brain, one cannot tell if Einstein ever entertained thoughts about its present condition, or even of Napoleon's penis. It is obvious that Einstein's brain entertained many thoughts. But what of Einstein's penis? Did it entertain anything? In Paris, France, Napoleon's penis lies in a jar. No one knows where the rest of Napoleon is, and if they do, it doesn't matter; they have his penis. Napoleon's brain is another question. Like his penis, it was present at all his great victories, his stunning defeats. But we don't have Napoleon's brain; the only brain we have is Einstein's. That means we have one brain and one penis; Napoleon's and Einstein's. We have these even though we can be said to have neither Einstein and Napoleon, Napoleon nor Einstein. It is usually the case that the possession of a man's brain presupposes the possession of the man; likewise, the appearance of a penis often indicates the presence of a man.

THE PARTY

Invite Don Rickles

THE FUTURE

The future arrives with a dogmatic
Gust of wind, ruining and changing
What is true and what will
Happen is never the same

The future is at my chin
Under the milk the bird
In my mouth points
To the future in my cereal

During the thunderstorm before
School as I pick up my alphabet
Mother steps in and out of the radio
With cinnamon toast

An! ode of! Buses and! the! future
Is! slipping into! itself like! a! red sleeve

Thad, a three-hundred pound man,
did not even feel like moving. Big Thad.

I am doing my report on Werner Heisenberg
And his principal of uncertainty. Werner
Heisenberg was a young German boy born in
1959 of an Italian sharecropper and a
Dynamo. He was born in 1959, the proud son
Of a shoemaker and an air balloon. Werner
Heisenberg, born in 1959, was the young son
Of a Jesuit and a coughdrop. The other kids
Did not like Werner, they were known to have
Affectionately referred to him as "Werner."
Of ancient Swiss heritage, Werner was born
Of two happy parents in the year 1959. Werner
Heisenberg is famous for his development of the
Heisenberg uncertainty principal. His roots
Lie in 1959, when he was born of two very shy
Teen-age equestrians. Werner grew up in the
50s, a time of great political strife and
Scientific upheaval, which serves as the
Colorful backdrop for his unprecedented
Accomplishments, the first of which was
His dynamic, pulse-arresting birth in 1959
In an obscure province of Hungaria. He went
On to formulate the principle of uncertainty,
Bearing his name, which has become the turning
Point of modern physics. When receiving one
Of his illustrious awards, Heisenberg replied,
"I know only that I was born in 1959, of Scotch
Weevils and shoeblack." Werner Heisenberg remains
One of the most alluring figures in the phenomenon
We call modern science. Although he rose from

Relative obscurity, the antsy son of a village
Priest and a thumbtack, he soon assumed a position
Of envy within the hierarchy of phenomena we call
Modern science. Accused of plagiarism and dilettantism,
Heisenberg baffled his opponents with ground
Breaking theories of nutrition and waste management,
Proving irrefutably that his genius was not limited
To the sterile halls of the laboratory. Although
These theories have proven unverifiable, they cast
A dark shadow of mystery and intrigue upon the life
And work of this seminal man. Even at the heights of
His inestimable achievements, Werner Heisenberg
Never forgot his humble past. Always approachable,
Seldom melodramatic, aimlessly poignant; this is how
Werner Heisenberg shall be remembered.

TOUCHDOWN TO COLLEGE!

Playing foot ball tot me to trust
my teammates and not only them butt
the foot ball itself would not
burst into spirals of most delicious
heat units

a thousand cocoa beans

II   THE GOLDEN AGE

BLOODMOBILE
SCHEDULE

The schedule for the American Red Cross Bloodmobile is as follows:

* Today from 1 to 4 a.m. at the American Legion Hall, 215 East Gravel Road. (free turkey slice)

* Tomorrow from 8 a.m. to noon at Dove of Peace Lutheran Church, 666 Roller Coaster Road, and 8:30 to 10:30 a.m. at St. Mark's United Methodist Church, 1431 Tombstone.

* Thursday from 10 p.m. at Monster Truck Show.

* Friday from 9:30 a.m. to 1:30 p.m. at Saffron High School, 734 11th Street, Saffron. (To give blood, high school students must be at least 70 years old and present a singed red parent.) Also, at Fun City 1599 W. Rancho Pancho Blvd., in the vomitorium, 9:33 a.m. to 9:34 a.m.; 2 a.m. - 5 a.m. joy ride.

* Saturday: no drives scheduled.

* Sunday at Dove of Peace Church, 7 a.m. I.V. rosary; 10 a.m. collection bowl.

* Monday: blush.

When I began swimming at this location I enjoyed the effects of your underwater fountains. The water propelled from below the gutters produced a stimulating massage effect. The pool itself and its caretakers deserve applause. I always feel safe and secure in this environment. The snacks in your snack bar are healthy and stimulating. They are not what we think of when we think of snacks, as per television advertisements. They are healthy and stimulating. I particularly enjoy the water droplet crudité. Until swimming in this pool I made only one swimsuit available to myself although that suit was ragged, blue, baggy and hopelessly out of style. I had purchased it several years before in a discount store on Fifth Avenue and 19th street. Although I was not swimming at that time, I had a well-paying job and saw through my past inactivity with an idea of healthfulness. Eventually I did lose weight. I would dive in and the thing would whip down around my ankles in the early morning. Early winter morning, the steam above the surface hardly visible in yellow pool light. The waist strings frayed and my waistband flickered from tightening the thing meticulously above my hip bones. Now I have a golden bikini. The radioactive lycra fibers of the suit weave together so as to constrict the purple skin of a ripe plum covered with cold beads of sweat, bursting from the inside pink sour nova. When I swim up from the bottom up and across my body swivels like a rifled bullet, giving off blades of light. I have noticed the nervousness of the staff, the high-strung command to clear the pool when this happens. I have noticed the way my little golden suit sucks up all the light and sun leaving a black sky full of airless clouds. I have felt the water over my skin, and heard the cracks of willows shattered by lightning. I have seen the poured concrete of the pool's keel crush itself as the ground opens up below and the water plummets in fifty meter hoops, counter-clockwise. I have seen the children drop their popsicles. I have seen mothers abandon their children. I have seen young women running ungracefully, tearing off their clothes and hair. I have heard the carbonated swoosh of the eclipse, the unpredicted eclipse that occurred when I dove from the highboard the instant my golden suit broke the surface of the still water.

THE PRIZE

I don't win the prize—
I call up Charles and we decide to meet
Charles also fails to win the prize. I get together
Some poetry and get on the train. When I get to 168ᵗʰ street
I get off and walk up to 179ᵗʰ and Charles
"Hi Charles"
Charles says hi. "Can I get you a drink?"
"Sure, I'll have a glass of Coke. Would you like
Some of my orange juice?" Charles politely refuses
Charles' room is very nice, the walls are covered
With colorful and witty collages he himself makes
"I like them," I say
"Thank you," he replies
"So who wants to go first?"
"I'll go first," says Charles
Charles reads a good short piece in a mellow voice
"That was good"
"Really?"
"Yes—I like the blue magnets," I tell him
"Yeah" Charles smiled, "Now you read"
"O.K."
I read a long poem in a mellow voice
"Wow" says Charles, shaking his head
"That was good"
"Oh yeah?"
"Yeah. Was that 'neurofelons'?"
"Yeah" I chuckle, "neurofelons"
"Hey listen to this"
Then Charles reads another poem
"Good stuff"
"You like it?"

"Yeah, I like it. That's very good how you use colors,
Colors and images and sounds"
"Thanks. Now you read"
"O.K. buddy"
I read a poem
I look up and Charles is on the edge
Of his bed, looking off nowhere
Nodding his head, he waits and murmurs
"Very good, very good. That was a good poem"
"You serious?"
"Yeah, I'm serious. There's something about the way
You use sounds and images, it's good"
After more we get tired of reading
I just put on my scarf and I put on my hat
And leave. I finally find someone on the street
Who will tell me where the subway is. I get there
And wait for the elevator to take me to track level
The elevator pulls up and I get in and there is only
Me and the elevator man and a woman pressed up against him
They whisper without moving their lips
And tilt their heads infinitesimally

There is no sound as she crinkles her hand
Around his blue uniform and he tells her goodbye
The woman is very black, parched, small next to him
She looks too attractive for a fat guy like him
He moves the lever down and tilts his cap
"This city no good." I look up. "No, this city
Is no place for a man"
"Tell me about it," I say
"There are too many women here and not enough men,
They wear a man out, you know?"
"Right on, man"

He picks at grey frizz on his scalp—"and violence,
Dirt and violence"
"Yeah" I say
"You go to college?"
"Yeah"
"I used to go, but the money ran out
The money's good here, but it's no place,
Nowhere for a man to be"
"Yeah"
"Every day more violence
More violence and more dirt,
I'm gonna leave, no place for a man to be"
The elevator door opens. I shake his hand
His eyes are half-closed and watery
"Yeah" I say, "yeah, yeah, yeah"

EX-PATRIOT

"First Day of Spring" is but a name
        as cold days continue

Forgive me for not writing for such a long time.

I wish you much happiness,
In this time of piercing cold

I have sent you a small present. I hope you like it.

This may be asking too much of you

I believe you have seen it on TV and the like, but
    seeing it in person is really something else.

I realize it would be a nuisance to you, but could you
    possibly help me find an apartment?

I shall contact you by phone later.

I trust that everyone has been doing well recently.
I'm afraid I haven't written for some time, but I'm
    doing well.

In this time of bright green

I'm busy everyday with both my studies and recreation

I am very happy
I am very thankful
I would like to visit you and offer my thanks

I have a favor to ask of you
I'll be staying at the Imperial Hotel until May 10
I'd really like to get together and chat with you.

The cherry trees have started to blossom;

Would you be so kind as to come at least this once?
I'll have beer and a light meal ready.

Mornings and nights have become quite chilly.

I apologize for not writing at all since graduation.

    I was very happy when I read this morning's
paper about your winning your first award in the
Shun'yo Exhibit. I offer you sincere congratulations.

    When I saw your paintings in your living
room the other day, even an amateur like me
could see how excellent they are.

    It's only natural that you won. I wish
you continued success in your work.

    My name is Hanna Hamilton.

What I did was completely inexcusable.

I deeply apologize.

I apologize again.

Next time you have a day off, we should get together
    to play tennis.

It continues to be bitterly cold. How are you doing?

Yesterday I met Mr. Yoshino, whom you kindly
    introduced to me, and consulted with him
    about many things.

I sincerely hope that he has great happiness
    in the next life.

Fall has deepened day by day.

I have started going to a fitness club.

Please don't hold this against me.

Hoping you have lifelong happiness

I'm afraid this is really presumptuous of me—

Please reply as soon as possible

Forgive my omission of formalities as I send this
    announcement

        It continues to be bitterly cold.

The other day I read your book *Thoughts on
    Postwar Japan*. Included with the book
    is "Making Apple Snacks," a pamphlet
    put out by my parents' apple orchard.
    It was of great help to me.
    My reading skills have quickened.

It rains every day

Happy New Year

I wish to thank you for all your help while I
    was in Japan

Breathing the mountain air after such a long
    time really refreshed me.

I send it to you as a token of my gratitude.

It's a local specialty, so please try it.

Please forgive me for sending this letter
    without any prior notice

In this time when the fresh grass glistens

We would like to sponsor a lecture gathering
at the university festival. In this regard, we really
would like to have you give a talk centering on
the way Japan's financial policies ought to be, if
this would be OK with you.

There are still days with cold winds
Please don't hold this against me.

I plan to visit your office in the near future

In addition to your showing me all sorts of
    folkcrafts, I feel as though I've gained
    a better understanding of pottery

It rains everyday

This year is quickly coming to a close

I ask that you please continue to favor
  me with your guidance

Be sure to invite me next time you go somewhere

Lastly, in wishing you health and success

  I announce my return to my country

I will take the liberty

  of calling you

    with regard to

      the time and place

Shootout at the OK Coral
Where blood and bubbles rise
To the surface and black powder
Scatters among reefs

"Ohhh Kayyy p-p-p-pardner . . . <glug>"

The wicked burp of six-guns
Hot lead cleaving seaweed
Johnny falling through a school
Of rainbow trout, lead harpoons

My studies lead me to posit
The existence of a dominant gunslinger
Around 1879—why else the disappearance
Of the Nautilus Gang?
The Mohawk Sharks?
The underwater blood covered faucets?
It led me from this armchair
In wetsuit underwear
To where I found 100% proof
Whiskey and the pearl-
Handled 88-notch 7-shot revolver of
Doc Cousteau, master of the slow draw
Wearer of the five gallon hat
And fringe-gill jacket
Lawbringer, underwater wagon pioneer
Bane of all sea horse thieves

Fupp! Fupp! He shot the eyes

Out of Billy the Squid

Tailed Butch Bassy and the Sunfish Kid

WHO WOULD WIN

Ernie Shavers vs. Ernie Hemingway—who would win???

Norman Mailer vs. Norman Bates—who would win???

Betty vs. Veronica—who would win???

Jacques Cousteau vs. Jacques Strap—who would win???

Yellow vs. Blue—who would win???

Blue vs. Gruyère—who would win???

The 60s vs. the 90s—who would win???

Those in their 60s vs. those in their 90s—who would win???

Andre Breton vs. Andre Champagne—who would win???

William Shatner vs. Gil Gerard—who would win???

World War I vs. World War II—who would win???

Ironsides vs. Columbo—who would win???

Columbo (the private detective) vs. Colombo (Sri Lanka)—who would win???

Julius Erving vs. Irving Goodman—who would win???

Dialectical Hegemony vs. Axiological Heterogeneity—who would win???

Herman Melville vs. Herman Munster—who would win???

Corbett vs. Courbet—who would win???

Merlin Olson vs. Merlin—who would win???

Sugar Ray Leonard vs. Leonard Nimoy—who would win???

Ginger vs. Marianne—who would win???

Arnold Schwarzenegger vs. Zimbabwe—who would win???

Alfredo Evangelista vs. Linda Evangelista—who would win???

Gurkhas vs. Gherkins—who would win???

Those who are concerned with who would win
                    vs.
Those who are not concerned with who would win—who would win???

I AM YAN SHAOHUA

I am Yan Shaohua

I am already

I have been already in the New York Estate

I lived in I lived in the uh

   Park Central Hotel

Park Central Hotel

   Very near from here, OK?

Please uh

   Let me see

My room telephone number is yeah

       My number is

247-8000 OK?

Please call back

As soon as possible, OK?

Or—or you can drive here

I am I'll have a meeting now

The address is the Perry Hotel

   P-I-E-R-R-E Hotel

P-I-E-R-R-E Hotel

   Maybe ten minutes from your unit

OK, it's very near, OK?

My room number is 15 40

My hotel address is Park Central Hotel

   870 7th Ave-nue at 56th Street

The telephone number is 247-eight thousand

   And my room is 1-5-4-0

OK, please call me back

Now I mean the Perry Hotel
  P-I-E-R-R-E Hotel
      It's very near from your unit
      OK? Bye bye.

FILM RETROSPECTIVE

FRANKIE AND JOHNNY (1965)
F&J Pictures/UA
Director: Frederick De Cordova

Max Von Sydow . . . . JOHNNY
Donna Douglas . . . . FRANKIE
Harry Morgan . . . . CULLY
Sue Anne Langdon . . . . MITZI
Nancy Kovack . . . . NELLY BLY
Audrey Christie . . . . PEG
Robert Strauss . . . . BLACKIE
James Milhollin . . . . PROPRIETOR OF COSTUME SHOP
Henry Corden . . . . GYPSY
Dave Willock . . . . PETE
Richard J. Reeves . . . . MAN ON STREET

FREAKY FRIDAY (1977)
Buena Vista/Disney
Director: Gary Nelson

Barbara Harris . . . . ELLEN ANDREWS
Jodie Foster . . . . ANNABEL ANDREWS
Max Von Sydow . . . . BILL ANDREWS
Patsy Kelly . . . . MRS. SCHMAUSS
Vicki Schreck . . . . VIRGINIA
Dick van Patten . . . . HAROLD JENNINGS
Sorrell Brooke . . . . MR. DILK
Ruth Buzzi . . . . OPPOSING COACH
Dick Von Sydow . . . . CASHIER

CHASTITY (1969)
AIP
Director: Alessio de Paola

Cher . . . . CHASTITY
Barbara London . . . . DIANA MIDNIGHT
Stephen Whittaker . . . . EDDIE
Tom Nolan . . . . TOMMY
Max Von Sydow . . . . CAB DRIVER
Joe Light . . . . MASTER OF CEREMONIES

HELL IN THE PACIFIC (1945)
Tristar/Sony
Director: Akira Ogata

Peter Cushing . . . . LT. COL. SMORGASBORD
Colleen Dewhurst . . . . GIRL ON BOAT
Max Schmeling . . . . SIDE-CAR GUNNER
Piper Laurie . . . . AUNT AGATHA
Mako . . . . PIANIST
Jill Ireland . . . . WAC #1
Burt Ward . . . . KAMIKAZE PILOT
Trevor Howard . . . . U-BOAT CAPTAIN

(lighting by Max Von Sydow)

THE BLACK BIRD (1975)
Columbia
Director: David Giles

George Segal . . . . SAM SPADE, JR.
Stephanie Audran . . . . ANNA KEMIDON
Lionel Stander . . . . IMMELMAN
Lee Patrick . . . . EFFIE
Elisha Cook, Jr. . . . . WILMER
Signe Hasso . . . . DR. CRIPPEN
Max Von Sydow . . . . HAWAIIAN THUG
Connie Kreski . . . . DECOY GIRL

CHE! (1969)
20th Century-Fox
Director: Richard Fleischer

Omar Sharif . . . . CHE GUEVARA
Max Von Sydow . . . . FIDEL CASTRO
Cesare Danova . . . . RAMON VALDEZ
Robert Loggia . . . . FAUSTINO MORALES
Barbara Luna . . . . ANITA MARQUEZ
Linda Marsh . . . . EVITA PERON
Max Von Sydow . . . . FULGENCIO BATISTA
Frank Silvera . . . . GOATHERD
Richard Angarola . . . . COL. SALAZAR

AIDA (1954)
Eagle Films (Italy)
Director: Clemente Fracassi

Sofia Loren . . . . AIDA, sung by Renata Tebaldi
Lois Bonhomme . . . . AMNERIS, sung by Ebe Stignanai
Luciano Della Maria . . . . RADAMES, sung by Max Von Sydow
Yul Brynner . . . . RAMSES, sung by Croce Iani

MY NAME IS NOBODY (1965)
Orion
Director: Jules Savate

Max Von Sydow . . . . PROF. NED BRAINARD/ROBOTIC BLOB
Erna Morena . . . . MA
Huntz Hall . . . . ROY BEAN
Sondra Locke . . . . THE BLONDE
Mac Davis . . . . MARTIAN LEADER
Gilles Queant . . . . GRAMPAW
Rhonda Fleming . . . . REDHEAD
Keye Luke . . . . GAS STATION ATTENDANT

THE SECRET SHARER (1960)
Hollywood Films
Director: Sam Peckinpah
AKA: "MY SHARING SELF"

Max Von Sydow . . . . CAPTAIN
Scatman Crothers . . . . LEGGAT
Patrick McGoohan . . . . CAPTAIN OF THE SEPHORA
Jerry Lewis . . . . FIRST MATE
Ben Vereen . . . . CABIN BOY
William Smith . . . . FIRST MATE OF SEPHORA
Lon Chaney . . . . STRANGLED CORPSE
Lucille Le Sueur . . . . CAPTAIN'S WIFE

BLACK CAESAR (1973)
MVS Productions
Director: Max Von Sydow

Max Von Sydow . . . . TOMMY GIBBS
Max Von Sydow . . . . JOE WASHINGTON
Max Von Sydow . . . . HELLEN
Max Von Sydow . . . . MR. LOCKE
Max Von Sydow . . . . CARDOZA
Max Von Sydow . . . . MOMMA GIBBS
Max Von Sydow . . . . CRAWDADDY

LOVE ME LONG (1983)
Cahuenga & Delongpre Films
Director: Skip Long

Esther Ralston . . . . LEILA LAMBERT
Alexander Kirkland . . . . HENRY CAMERON
Peter North . . . . MAN ON PHONE
Lisa Lipps . . . . X-RAY TECHNICIAN
Maxx Von Sydow . . . . TRUCKER

(All Films Shown at Twilight)

When I hear the word "culture" I reach for my revolver
When I hear the word "stamen" I reach for my pistil
When I hear the word "gadfly" I reach for my wallflower
When I hear the word "onomatopoeia" I reach for my recitative
When I hear the word "truck" I reach for my life
When I hear the word "travesty" I reach for my three-piece suit
When I hear the word "elbow" I reach for my concussion
When I hear the word "goatee" I reach for my Remington Microscreen
When I hear the word "insight" I reach for my flagon
When I hear the word "doughnut" I reach for my doughnut
When I hear the word "religion" I reach for my erection
When I hear the word "elephant" I reach for my blunderbuss
When I hear the word "apocalypse" I reach for my index cards
When I hear the word "sustenance" I reach for my apiary
When I hear the word "idea" I reach for my dumbbells
When I hear the word "establishment" I reach for my kerosene
When I hear the word "Rosencranz" I reach for my . . .
When I hear the word "glass" I reach for my eyeball
When I hear the word "greatness" I reach for my footnote
When I hear the word "beauty" I reach for my cutlass
When I hear the word "dishonor" I reach for my intestines
When I hear the word "constitution" I reach for my congestion
When I hear the word "remorse" I reach for my children
When I hear the word "debonair" I reach for my wholesale
                     furniture warehouse
When I hear the word "peachy" I reach for my Solzhenitsyn
When I hear the word "baby" I reach for my comeback
When I hear the word "fire" I reach for my butterfly collection
When I hear the word "maniac" I reach for my swim cap and goggles
When I hear the word "insolence" I reach for my villa

When I hear the word "faith" I reach for my ambergris
When I hear the word "electronics" I reach for mis compadres
When I hear the word "quintessence" I reach for your brother,
                                        the genius
When I hear the word "work" I reach for my gaskets
When I hear the word "reincarnation" I reach for my palm
When I hear the word "midnight" I reach for my big sisters

AMBITION

When music moves away
   From dance, atrophy sets in

When poetry moves away
   From music, atrophy sets in

I want one of those
   Trophies

III   CONTEMPORARIES

1706   Born in Boston, January 12 (January 6, 1705, Old Style) on Milk Street near Old South Church; baptized with milk.

1707   Enters Boston Grammar School, and after a year is sent to private school.

1709   Assists his father, a candlemaker.

1711   Apprenticed to his brother James as a printer's assistant.

1712   Breaks his indenture and travels to Philadelphia, where he finds employment with Samuel Keimer, a denture maker.

1713   At the frantic urging of Governor Keith, leaves for London in November with James Ralph.

1714   Employed in London.

1715   Unemployed in London.

1718   Leaves for Philadelphia July 11[1], with Mr. Denham, a Philadelphia merchant, who later employs Franklin as his son.

1719   Ages.

1727   While returning to Keimer's shop via ferryboat, pulls drowning man from rough waters into boat by hair. Both realize it is more important to live than die.

1728   Purchases Keimer's paper, *The Universal Instructor*, begins its publication as *The Gazelle*; opens and closes various shoppes.

1729   Assists his father, a candlemaker.

1730   Learns to read. Appointed Public Printer by Assembly of Pennsylvania.

1731   Fornicates.

1732   Begins *Poor Richard's Almanac* (3 AM).

---

[1] "Leaving Day," a British national Holiday since 1789.

1733–44 Years of public service as "first citizen" of Philadelphia—founds Union Fire Company, publishes *Treatise on Asbestos*, is appointed Deputy Postmaster-General, invents the "Franklin Stove," begins work on crockery, plans city police, establishes alternate system of real numbers, pulls eyelid over eye to evacuate dust, christens American Philosophical Society.

1745   Assists his father, a candlemaker.

1746   Begins researches in electricity (3 AM).

1748   Retires from active participation in printing and publishing. Treated at Philadelphia General for ink poisoning and smoke inhalation.

1749   Piano lessons.

1751   Subsists entirely on cheeses.

1753   Awarded the Copley Lightning Bolt of the Royal Society of London for his research into the nature of electricity.

1754   Serves as a Commissioner from Pennsylvania to the Albany Colonial Congress, where he proposes a plan for serving lavish desserts.

1755–56 Assists in raising supplies for Braddock's expedition; assists in consuming such supplies; supervises construction of forts in Pennsylvania; supervises construction of ports in Transylvania; serves in the field as an ear of corn.

1757   Appointed clotting agent for the Province of Pennsylvania, sails for London.

1762   Returns to Pennsylvania. Published: *Remarks on the Slowness of Ships*.

1764   Again sails for London as representative of The Pennsylvania Electric Company. Charged with emotions.

1765–70 In London, hangs around in lobbies and doorways. Visits Germany and France, and is appointed agent for Georgia, New Jersey, and Massachusetts.

1771   Begins writing autobiography (3 AM).

1774   Turns 68[2]—throws simultaneous birthday parties in France, Germany, and New Jersey, during which he poses the question to his guests: "What good have I done today?"

1775   Returns to America. Suffers from abnesia; member of Philadelphia Committee of Safety, one of Pennsylvania's delegates to the Second Continental Congress, and member of the Committee of Secret Correspondence. Forms precocious but short lived Philadelphia Committee of Space Exploration.

1776   Drafts Declaration of Independence; forms the new United States of America. Arrives in Paris in December.

1778   Signs treaty for French alliance with United States in invisible ink.

1779   Appointed U.S. Minister Plenipotentiary to France.

1780   Gesticulates wildly.

1783   With John Jay and John Adams, signs the Treaty of Paris, ending the American Revolution. Abides in Residence Halls.

1784   In retirement at Passy, resumes his scientific interests and the writing of his autobiography. Plays chess and consumes bagatelles from sunrise to sunset.

1785   Resigns his diplomatic post and returns to Philadelphia, where he is chosen President of Pennsylvania; re-elected in 1786 and 1787.

1787   Begins mass production and sale of "Bottled Lightning," is rumored to consult with winged creatures and interlopers.

1788   Retires from public life; appears only momentarily in trenchcoats.

1789   Assists his father, a candlemaker.

1790   Dies April 17. On April 21, is buried in the yard of Christ Church at Fifth and Arch Streets, Philadelphia, after a funeral procession witnessed by the entire population of the United States.

[2] 69, Old Style

FRIENDSHIP

We rode our bikes up the mountains
Along the beach and as the sun
Set into downtown Santa Barbara
Weaving through the cars and shoppers
I really liked that, it was like
The end of a life

A MAN OF LETTERS

I am a man of letters:
A, B, D, G, O, & P.

This is my pad,
where you may find my dog, Bap,
whose teeth form a gap,
and my god. My voice comes from
the pagoda, where I am struggling
with a bad bag. Please excuse this mess of books—
Or take a look: I'm reading *The Poems of Do Po;*
Bad Pod, a sci-fi novel about
bean travel; and *Go Boa Go!,* an
inspirational tale about a snake.

LIFE OF GAME

I was born into this really fun game
Called "life"—you try to stay alive
As long as you can. It's not easy
Because there are so many things
That can happen. One of the neatest
Things about this game of living
Is that there are many games
Within it like the money game
The sex game and the thinking
Game. At this point in my life
I'm losing the money game, winning
The sex game, and not playing
The thinking game too much. One
Of the neatest things about these
Games within the game is that everything
Can change so fast and drastically
So that you never really know
How you're doing. This is part
Of the pleasure and the pain of the game.
Some come to the game half-heartedly
Some wildly; some play on in a daze.
Another neat thing about this game
Is that what happens in the game
Really happens to you. Like if you're
Playing the money game driving a fast
Luxury car and there is an accident
In which you lose an arm *you really*
Lose an arm. Or after playing the sex
Game for a while you find your
Eyes on a new little player.
Another crazy aspect of this game

I really like but sometimes can't understand
Is that you'll be playing one game, say
The sex game, and at some point it turns
Out to be the money game you've been
Playing all along. As I said, things can get
Confusing, but on a weekday
Or a weekend night there's really
Nothing more amusing.

INTERVIEWS

(1)

A: What disturbs you?

B: The fact that I have a skeleton inside.

A: May your anxiety be applicable to other forms
        of art?

B: First, it should be noted that anxiety itself is a form of art, and that I am not
        concerned with forms.

A: You have developed a reputation in your interviews for becoming evasive—how
        do you respond?

B: Would you rather I become a vase? Or jump in a pond? I feel that I am as
        necessary as my face.

A: What are your thoughts on control and merit?

B: Merit has its badges, while control is another form of emptiness.

A: Scholars have wrangled over whether you are a nationalist or a sensationalist . . .

A: What do you think of the weak?

B: Five days is never enough—five teeth cannot fill a mouth—let us have 20–28
        day weeks.

(2)

Q: What would you do if you got $10,000?

64

A: I dunno. Maybe I go somewhere else.

Q: Where?

A: Puerto Rico—you know—it's been twenty years. Twenty years, never been there.

Q: What is that you're eating?

A: Lot a stuff.

Q: Yeah, but what?

A: Mac and cheese. Potato. Spinach. Chicken. Rolls.

Q: Where'd you get it?

A: Julio said he's hungry. He calls on the phone. Mike said fix him up too. So hey, I said Julio fix me up too.

Q: They fixed you up, huh.

A: Yeah (smiles).

Q: Would you do that (bunji jumping)?

A: No-o-o-o.

Q: No? Why not? Would you do it for money?

A: (Pause) Yeah.

Q: How much?

A: I dunno . . . a hundred, two hundred dollars.

Q: What about an airplane, how much to jump out of an airplane?

A: No, I don't do that.

Q: Not for a thousand?

A: Huh-uh.

Q: Ten-thousand?

A: No way, no.

(3)

A: What kind of music do you listen to?

B: Philosophy.

A: You've mentioned, in other interviews, having studied with those who believe, quote, "there is only one story." What implication, if any, has this so-called "literary monotheism" for your work and religious politics?

B: Yes.

A: How does the way you speak relate to words?

B: I cherish words. This affects my voice. It's not usage. Sometimes I am speakless. Logic. Mimicry. Imitation. Outcry.

A: Would you say this is systematic?

B: Nothing could be further from the truth. After I wrote *Boogaloo Volts* some students approached me—this was during the 60s when such systematic approaches were widely denigrated—and I told them I was concerned only with truth in its manifold forms. This incident, you may recall, was the basis for my stained-glass piece "Vinny."

A: This is another facet—would you say you have been accepted by the community of fine artists?

B: There is a mutual lack of disrespect.

A: Say something about your children's works.

B: All of us, we are children.

CURB VICTIM

A curb victim speaks out on his emotional and physical
Debilitation resulting from a brutal curbing incident
This hideous form of suburban amusement is spreading
It involves roaming gangs of youth accosting and
Holding down an innocent bystander
The victim's mouth is forced open
And placed on a cement street corner
As if to take a bite
The youths take turns
Until no teeth remain

KILLING MY PEN-PAL

I plan an escape as I would plan
To take off my clothes
That is, there isn't much planning
I just undress and look in the mirror
From ancient times the mirror
Has been a symbol of nudity

I feel vulnerable, I may be killed
Or injured at any moment—this coupled
With the feeling that I might kill at any time
The person whose kitchen I'm in
Who tells me to cut the onion
"Persil," "Estragon"
"Feuilles de Laurier"
I find this comforting
And spend the night
In your kitchen

If you have been shocked you can shock
You carry a charge
This is not science
But the magic of being alive

The clever man wears idiot's clothing
(Although I love the idiot-sounding)
The intelligent man who portrays himself as a fool is stupid
The stupid fool who portrays himself as intelligent is a man
The portrayer who is stupid fools himself into intelligence
There is no stupidity in foolishness
The man who takes medicine is a fool (if not sick)
I prescribe a medicine ball for all afflictions,
                              including foolishness

Foolishness does not go well with tae kwon do
Describe a medicine ball and its cousin, the piñata

How silly, a home
Even an address is farfetched
Better to stand downtown
And stare at the numbers

    lie on the floor in a basement in Topeka
    take a shower in Amarillo
    kiss a pillow in Marlboro

All of this is better than a home
A self-deception, this home
A stranger is more native

Smile—I remembered the word
"Hermeneutics" all on my own
First I had to think of "exegesis"
And what I'm doing out here
In your spacious apartment
I wonder about my life
Is it moving in

Your address is an argument
I write for trombone
It cheers me up
It's a glass of water
In my wet pocket
Spilling up the stairs

I open my eyes as I would
Two jewelry boxes
Holding two engagement rings
For two intelligent women
I buy a tool box
And keep sweets in it

LOW DRONES

(DADO MORONI)

I love waking on cold mornings
with pieces of harpsichord hanging from the
roof gutter

This song belongs to my eyelid
at least these three notes

my life is rain
it comes down
softer than the universe

(who's Dado Moroni?)

(he's a harpsichord player)

(I'm not sure there's enough here)

(but what's here is something)

(refrain)

EXPLODED

I got a ton of vibes from Jennifer and Yun-Su
But I didn't really get any vibes from Christine
But that's O.K. cause I was giving a lot of vibes
To Jennifer. It's funny, I got a call from Ricardo
It's very subtle, how I approach the entire evening
I was trying to show myself off in a certain light
And they were getting into it. In the bagel shop
There were two policemen and I turned to Christine
And said, there's something to—then she put her
Hand over my mouth and said I love the way you talk—
I was thinking maybe. It wasn't so easy, we just

THE SO-CALLED GREENHOUSE EFFECT

1.

The dust laden wind on the Atlantic coast of Africa.
Damaging, Injurious. You might say I've been involved.
I have covered my neck with a band
In order to protect it from the sun, do you mind?
It is not a bag like a knapsack, and it is not likely
To bring about a vexatious or baffling situation.
This "thing" I have attached to my neck does resemble
A narrow strip of cloth sewn or glued by hand
To the extreme ends of the head, but it is in reality a far cry.
Similar attachments have often been used as gates
Controlling the water that flows from a horse's head.

2.

Yesterday I passed by a row of shrubs or trees.
I felt pleasure. I turned to Rick and said,
"The condition of those trees is marked by the
Sudden development of a nation or a nation-state."
Rick pointed to the horizon and said
"You have not yet acknowledged
The vivid god of electric light and thunder."

Rick is a tenor with a powerful dramatic voice well suited
To all this lush greenery.

TONIGHT

Tonight my girlfriend's brother
is visiting from Japan. We take
him to New York's tallest building—
the moon

FIRST MAN ON THE BED

It's inexpressible—I can only show you this photo of me planting
our flag among the sheets. The slight gravity of the bed allowed me to
hover a few minutes before falling asleep. Its surface was colder
than the Earth. A pillow I threw swirled out of distance as millions
of viewers sat entranced. I heard your radio transmissions. Eventually,
it was quiet enough to wake.

POEM FOR THE GOVERNMENT

I'm writing some poems for the government
but I can't talk about them now.
I can't talk at all. The writing has been going
well, on schedule, and all expenses have been taken
care of. I'm not at liberty to discuss
the secretive nature of my work
which demands that I write
in silence and disgust and under
an assumed name. My work for the government
is not only confidential, it is gross, exquisite
many lives hang in the balance. I'm also writing some poems
that aren't for the government, but now those seem
about nothing at all. I don't know where or how my poems
will be used, but I want them to be fool-
ish and deadly.

That I write in silence
and seclusion and under
this parasol, for the government
my tiny son at my feet, makes me
extremely poetic. I think
of splashes and hear the poems
I am writing in this paradise, one
of which is really for you
I include it in the government batch
perhaps to better include you in our lives.

LORENZO GUZMAN

Otro deportes:	herraduras, bolos, pesca con mosca
Actividades:	ajedrez, filológicos
Color Favorito:	verde
Número Favorito:	trece
Loción:	de todos
Mejor Mexicano:	Montalban
El Mejor en su peso:	Floyd Patterson
Nombre del padre:	Lacan
Nombre de la madre:	Lanzacohetes
Su ídolo:	Art Pepper
El Mejor Extranjero:	Veeraphol
Cicatrices:	No.
Mánager:	Kenzo Koch
Entrenador:	Juan Anderson
Zapatillas:	13
Platillo Favorito:	Pescado con moscas
Supersticios:	Sí.
Hijos:	una, Penita
Esposa:	separado
Campeonatos:	guantes de oro, de platino
Primer trabajo:	cocinero
Donde vive:	Hermosilla

Her legs look good in cream stockings
hot dogs bursting with flavor
Hot water in my ears

I check the mirror
I drive North
I fail to see the incomplete
I feel the anger of his fatness
I have always been afraid
I have seen my own mind
I have just come in from a crash
I leapt sideways into the cauldron of infinity
I like drinking cold water (clod atrew)
I line a funnel with velvet
I love the imagined brick layers of existence
I only speak German
I rejoice in your pleasant trees
I said "Bartender, Bartender, do you know who I am?"
I see nothing from my window
I sit here, a socialite
I spent the day in Ageloff Towers reading
I think the mattress
I wake up Sunday morning and walk through Chinatown
I walk to the satisfactory
I was slipping into a mild trance
If you know something, prove it
I'll have a severe mind-melt with tomato and cheese
I'm a veteran of some wars
I'm tired but I'm not going to waste
In a gold red noise of smell
In the middle of *Eraserhead*
In other words, wonderful, super, one
In the window of a diner
It is late, I have been grandsashing

It's a dark art
it's good to see flowers
it was a test

Jablonsky is dead then he is alive
Jon Anderson gave me this typewriter

Kabobs, souvlakis, coleslaws, chips

Ladies and gentlemen
little trees create a possibility that
Lonely debris bee canoli
Look how simple I am,

manila envelope: tufts of hair
Meditation fills us with the confidence to face
Mombasa – 9 AM – snake eyes
Mother, father, where are you now?
my fingers touch the knight
My love lake genteel bauble

Near a beautiful staircase, hand-wrought
Next to me, the cook
No man—only cartoon characters
No more of me somewhere,
Not thinking of clocks but the chime
Now hear this:
Now I'm waiting in a station

O Eggbert, shell of man
oblong, awkward
Of rose in steam
on a greyhound, most anonymous,
On phone to Madras Mahal:

On the B to Stillwell Avenue
On the divan between the lamps
On the way to the bus to Long Beach Blvd

Parting is such sweet sorrow
parts are missing and it doesn't make sense
Perhaps the adult is just a child

Scout is chasing deer
she cries before the flowers
She delicately fries the toast
Sleeping in my hood
stale pizza crust, two bottlecaps

Take pleasure in the failure
Talking all night with Bill Yokoyama
That would be me, a self-
The artist Don Powley
The crime boss' white car passes the waterboy's clear car
The lives of two
The method, generalized
The morning mist is thick as Saunders
The one by the piano, the mother and daughter
The saleswoman at Okadaya
There's a craziness
They gasped
Thick Belgian waffles
This is the end of all expectation
This is to the women of Texas,
This morning I played pinball
This was lovely snow falling, my plan
Through the lightning of my hometown
tiny quail eggs
To breathe again in the mist

to destroy anything,
Two juicy hamburgers in my hand

Unemployed in the poorest section of Flatbush
Upon visiting Max
Up the ramp past the Freak Show

We ate in the bathroom
What has been bothering you, my son
When did Schmitt die?
when the sun gathers
white grapes smashed by a purple hammer

You tell me you're fixing boilers
You were remembering

Zia—was out of country